A New True Book

BRAZIL

By Karen Jacobsen

Flag of Brazil

CHILDRENS PRESS®
CHICAGO

Dancer dressed for carnival

PHOTO CREDITS

© Victor Banks—29 (right)

Cameramann International Ltd.—2, 11 (left), 31 (bottom left), 39 (right), 43 (left)

© Victor Englebert—10 (2 photos), 14 (left top & bottom), 32 (right)

© Virginia Grimes—13 (top right)

Grolier Incorporated—6 (map)

Hillstrom Stock Photos—© Liz Veternik, 39 (top left)

Historical Pictures Service, Chicago—23 (left), 26, 27

© John M. Hunter for Reynolds Photographers—15, 24 (left), 33 (2 photos)

Chip and Rosa Maria de la Cueva Peterson—4 (2 photos), 11 (right), 13 (bottom right), 24 (right), 29 (left), 35, 36 (2 photos); © Brian L. Koster, 8 (top right); © Jim Martin, 16, 31 (top)

Photri—8 (bottom), 17, 20, 42

© Carl Purcell—31 (bottom, center, & right), 41 (bottom left)

© Reynolds Photographers—13 (left), 32 (left)

Root Resources—© Jane P. Downton, 39 (bottom left)

Shostal Associates—© K. Kummels, 14 (right), 21 (2 photos); © G. Ricatto, 45 (left)

Tom Stack & Associates—© Gary Milburn, 8 (top left); © Steve Martin, 8 (center); © Warren & Genny Garst, 18; © M. Timothy O'Keefe, 34 (left)

Tony Stone Worldwide-Click/Chicago—© Ed Rooney, Cover; © Elizabeth Harris, 34 (right), 41 (top); © Berlitz, 41 (bottom right), 43 (right); © John Star, 44; © Suzanne Murphy, 45 (right)

United Press International—28

Maps by Len W. Meents—7, 9, 14, 15, 20, 23

Cover — Rio de Janeiro Botofogo Bay, Sugar Loaf Mountain

Library of Congress Cataloging-in-Publication Data

Jacobsen, Karen.
  Brazil / by Karen Jacobsen.
    p.   cm. — (A New true book)
  Includes index.
  Summary: An overview of the largest South American country, which includes its history, geography, and living conditions today.
  ISBN 0-516-01171-5
  1. Brazil—Juvenile literature.
[1. Brazil.] I. Title.
F2508.5.J33 1989
981—dc20

89-10042
CIP
AC

TABLE OF CONTENTS

Coffee, maize (corn), and soybeans are some of the products grown in Brazil.
The waterfront at Belém, at the mouth of the Amazon River (below)

BRAZIL OR BRASIL?

Almost 500 years ago, explorers from Portugal came to a new land. They found a special tree growing there. Its wood was used to make a bright red dye for cloth. In Portuguese the tree's name was *pau-brasil*. So the explorers named the new land Brasil for its special trees.

Today the nation's official name is *República Federativa*

BRAZIL

SOUTH AMERICA

ATLANTIC OCEAN

COLOMBIA

VENEZUELA

GUYANA

SURINAME

FRENCH GUIANA

GUIANA HIGHLANDS

Pico da Neblina

Boa Vista

Rio Negro

EQUATOR

Putumayo R.

Amazon

Javari River

Amazon River

Grand Opera House, Manaus

Manaus

Macapá

MARAJÓ

Belém

São Luís

Madeira River

Tapajós River

Xingu River

Tocantins R.

Teresina

Fortaleza

Cape São Roque

Natal

Pôrto Velho

Rio Branco

Guaporé River

MATO GROSSO PLATEAU

Cuiabá

Goiânia

Brasília

São Francisco River

BRAZILIAN HIGHLANDS

João Pessoa

Recife

Maceió

Aracaju

Salvador (Bahia)

Ilhéus

PERU

BOLIVIA

Corumbá

Paraguay R.

Araguaia River

Tocantins River

Belo Horizonte

Itabira

Conganhás

Pico da Bandeira

Vitória

Campos

PARAGUAY

TROPIC OF CAPRICORN

Londrina

Paraná River

Volta Redonda

Campinas

São Paulo

Santos

Niterói

Rio de Janeiro

Guaíra Falls

Iguazú Falls

ARGENTINA

CHILE

PACIFIC OCEAN

G. BUCTEL

Curitiba

Joinvile

Blumenau

Florianópolis

Uruguay River

Pôrto Alegre

URUGUAY

Pelotas

ATLANTIC OCEAN

N

Plaza of the Three Powers, Brasília

Cacao		Industry	
Cattle		Iron Ore	Fe
Citrus Fruit		Lumber	
Coffee		Sugar	
Cotton		Tobacco	

Miles
200 400 600 800

Kilometers
200 400 600 800 1000 1200

VENEZUELA
GUYANA
SURINAME
FRENCH GUIANA
COLOMBIA
ECUADOR
BRAZIL
Brasília
PERU
BOLIVIA
PARAGUAY
CHILE
URUGUAY
ARGENTINA

do Brasil or the Federative Republic of Brazil.

No matter how it is spelled, with an *s* or a *z*, the nation is a giant. It is the largest country in South America and the fifth largest in the world. Only the Soviet Union, China, Canada, and the United States are larger.

The Atlantic Ocean forms the long east coast of Brazil. Many nations share their boundaries with Brazil.

7

The slow-moving sloth (above left), passion-flowers (above right), and the St. Vincent Amazon parrot (right) are found in the jungles along the mighty Amazon River (below).

THE AMAZON REGION

The equator crosses Brazil just north of the Amazon River. The Amazon and the other rivers that run into it make up the world's largest river system.

Much of the land around the Amazon system is unexplored. Some of the world's most unusual plants and animals live in the rain forests and jungles of the Amazon.

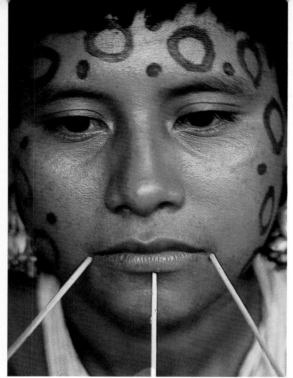

The Indians have lived in the Amazon rain forests for centuries.

Many Indians live on or near the northern and western branches of the Amazon river system. The Indians are able to find food and shelter in the wilderness.

Manaus is a city far up the Amazon River. It was built in

Trade travels up and down the Amazon River between the inland city of Manaus (left) and the port city of Belém (above).

the jungle almost one hundred years ago by wealthy rubber plantation owners. Many of the city's buildings were shipped in pieces from Europe. Even today, a trip up the Amazon River to Manaus can take several days.

11

THE NORTHEAST COASTAL REGION

The first settlers from Portugal settled on Brazil's northeast coast. They grew sugar, cotton, cacao, and tobacco. Slaves, brought from Africa, were forced to work on these plantations. The Portuguese grew wealthy by shipping crops from Brazil to Europe.

Today, there are no slaves in Brazil. But plantations are

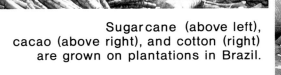

Sugarcane (above left),
cacao (above right), and cotton (right)
are grown on plantations in Brazil.

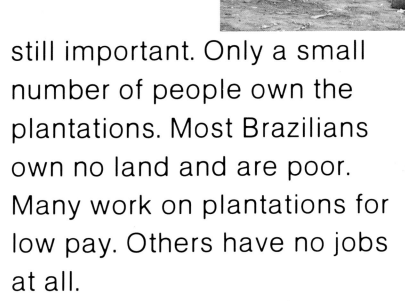

still important. Only a small
number of people own the
plantations. Most Brazilians
own no land and are poor.
Many work on plantations for
low pay. Others have no jobs
at all.

13

Square and Santo Antonio Church in Recife (above). Busy market (left) and street (above left) in Salvador.

The major northeastern cities are Salvador and Recife. From them, cotton, sugar, and other crops are shipped around the world.

THE SOUTHERN COASTAL REGION

Guiana Highlands

Marajó island

Amazon Region

Chapada de Mato Grosso

Brazilian Highlands

Great Escarpment

The southern half of Brazil has hills and mountains. Few early settlers moved inland because of the mountains. Instead, most people stayed along the coast, farming the rich soil and cutting lumber in the forests.

Coastal plain near the city of Vitória

Downtown São Paulo

Brasília
★

Rio de
Janeiro

São Paulo

Today, the southern coastal region is world-famous for growing coffee, Brazil's largest export crop. The modern cities of São Paulo and Rio de Janeiro on Brazil's east coast are the largest in Brazil.

São Paulo's skyscrapers are the centers of worldwide business activities.

Rio's museums, stores, and beaches attract tourists from everywhere.

Rio de Janeiro

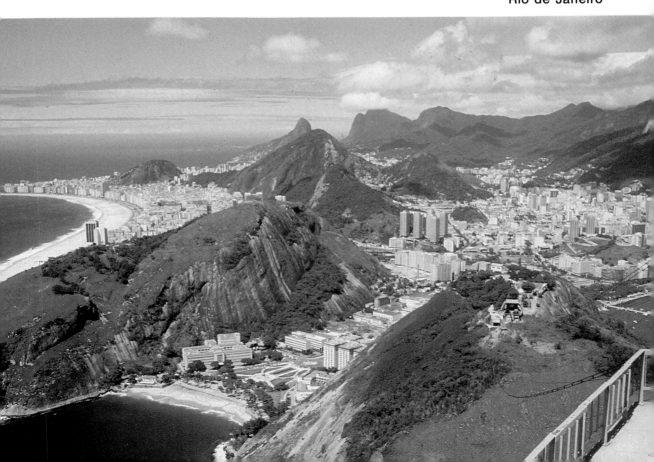

THE CENTRAL REGION

Miles from the ocean, on the border with Argentina, are the Iguaçu Falls. The falls are millions of years old. They are a part of the Río de la Plata river system and an important source of electric power for Brazil.

Iguaçu Falls

The central region is a frontier—a huge and sometimes dangerous place.

Most of central Brazil is hot and dry or hot and rainy. Deadly tropical diseases are a constant threat. But the land has many rich resources.

In recent years Brazilians have started to move there. New roads and improved communications, modern medicine, refrigeration, and air conditioning are making life there possible.

BRASÍLIA

Brasília, the capital city, is in central Brazil. In 1956 workers began to build Brasília in the wilderness. Today, it is a city of more than a million people. Its modern buildings house Brazil's government offices. Like a magnet, Brasília is pulling more people into the central region.

The Congress Building (above) and the cathedral at Brasília (below)

BRAZIL'S PAST

The discovery of South America caused trouble between Portugal and Spain. Each country wanted to own the new land. But, instead of going to war, the two countries agreed to divide South America into two parts. In 1494 a line was drawn. Portugal won the land east of the line. Spain got the land west of the line.

In 1500, Pedro Álvares Cabral was the first

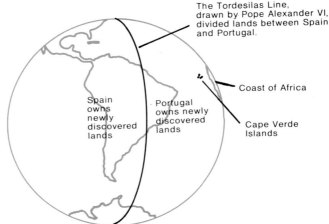

Spain owns newly discovered lands

Portugal owns newly discovered lands

Coast of Africa

Cape Verde Islands

Pope Alexander VI divided South America between Portugal and Spain by drawing a line down a map.

A carved portrait of Pedro Álvares Cabral (left)

Portuguese to explore Brazil's northeast coast. Thirty years later colonists from Portugal settled at Salvador. They hoped to find gold and jewels. Instead, they found that the land was good for growing sugar and other crops.

Gold (above) was discovered near Ouro Preto (left) in the 1690s.

Many years later, gold and diamonds were discovered inland from the coast. In the 1600s and 1700s fortune hunters came to search for hidden riches in the jungle.

THE EMPEROR OF BRAZIL

In 1807, the French army, led by Napoleon, invaded Portugal. The Portuguese king and his family fled to Brazil for their safety. They stayed until the French lost the war. Then, in 1821, the king returned to rule Portugal. His son, Prince Pedro, stayed behind to rule Brazil.

In 1822, Pedro declared Brazil independent from Portugal. The prince became

Dom Pedro II,
emperor of Brazil

Emperor Pedro I, but he was
not popular. Brazil's leaders
forced him to give up his
throne. They made his five-
year-old son the new ruler. In
1841, the young boy became
Dom Pedro II, emperor
of Brazil.

Dom Pedro II ruled Brazil
for almost fifty years. He

supported the building of
many roads, railroads, and
telegraph lines in Brazil. In
1888 he abolished slavery.
This made the slave owners
angry. They forced Dom
Pedro II to leave Brazil. The
slave owners declared Brazil
to be a republic, and took
over the government.

Slave labor was used on Brazilian plantations.

In 1943 Getúlio Vargas, left, the president of Brazil, met with Franklin D. Roosevelt, the president of the United States, to discuss war issues.

In both World Wars, Brazil sided with the United States and its allies against Germany. Then, in 1945, Brazil became a founding member of the United Nations.

During the 1950s, Brazil

Huge dams, such as the one at Itaipu (above), and giant hydroelectric stations, such as the one at Paulo Afonso Falls (left), bring electrical power to all parts of Brazil.

grew rapidly. Power plants were built. Factories were started. In 1957 a nuclear reactor began operating in São Paulo. In 1960 the government moved to Brasília, the new capital city.

Then, in 1964, military leaders took power in Brazil. They made their own laws and grew rich. The Brazilian people lost many of their rights and grew poorer.

But, in 1985, there was a change. A civilian president was elected. The people gained more power. In 1988 a new Constitution became law. It guarantees more rights for all Brazilians.

THE PEOPLE OF BRAZIL

There are more than 140 million Brazilians. The Indians were the first people of Brazil. But, for hundreds of years, other people have been coming to Brazil. The Portuguese

People from Italy, Germany, Japan, Lebanon, Syria, and many other countries have made Brazil their home.

came as settlers, and
Africans came as slaves.
Today, most Brazilians are
Indian and Portuguese,
Indian and African, or
African and Portuguese.
Many Brazilians are a
mixture of all three.

Most Brazilians are a mixture of races.

Crowded streets of Porto Alegre (left) and
a village street in Brazil (right)

LIFE IN BRAZIL

More than half of Brazil's
people live in cities. The rest
live in villages, on the
plantations, near mining
camps, or in other remote
places.

Indian hut (left) in the Amazon and a simple farm home in Crato (right)

In areas that have a hot, dry climate, houses are made of stone or plaster with tile roofs. In rainy, humid climates, many Indian families build houses from palm leaves, tree branches, and mud. They sleep in hammocks hung from posts.

Because the climate in almost every part of Brazil is very warm, most people wear lightweight clothing year-round. People who work outside often wear very little.

But Brazilian cowboys, called *gauchos*, must wear

This gaucho wears special clothes to protect his body. He carries a comb, not a gun, in his holster.

special clothing to protect
them against the burning
sun, biting insects, and
rough bushes on the cattle
range.

In Brazil's cities, people
live in high-rise buildings or
in single-family houses. The
poor people live in slums
called *favelas*.

The government is trying

In many cities, poor people look through garbage (left) to find food and items to sell. Houses in the *favelas* (right) are made from scraps of cardboard and tin.

to create more jobs and
improve housing for poor
people.

The government also
wants to help Brazilians
living outside the cities. It
is selling some land to the
poor. For the first time, these
people will be able to
grow their own crops on their
own land for their own profit.

Much of the government
land is in the central and
Amazon regions. It has never
been farmed before. The
people who go to live there
are true pioneers.

EDUCATION IN BRAZIL

About half of Brazil's people are under eighteen years old. Many of them never have the chance to go to school. They are too poor, or live in parts of Brazil where there are no schools to attend.

Millions of children attend school for only a few years. Then they must go to work.

Those students who can afford to go to school attend eight years of primary

Good schools are found in the cities, but it is harder to find teachers and schools in the rural parts of Brazil.

school, followed by four years of high school. Only a small number of students are able to go on to Brazil's universities and technical colleges.

BRAZIL'S RESOURCES

Brazil has deposits of gold and precious stones. It has iron and other metal ores. But it has very little oil to turn into gasoline fuel. Instead of buying oil from other countries, Brazil turns sugarcane plants into alcohol to use as fuel. Making alcohol fuel has created thousands of jobs for Brazilians and saved billions of cruzados. (*Cruzado* is the name for the unit of money of Brazil.)

FOOD FROM BRAZIL

Tapioca is made from the manioc root.

Brazil produces a wonderful variety of food crops for sale to other countries. It is the world's largest producer of coffee and orange juice. Tropical fruits, Brazil nuts, sugar,

Lobsters from the sea and fresh fruits and vegetables are found in city markets.

beef, and fish are also important exports.

Brazilians—rich, poor, young, old, city dwellers, or country folk—have much to enjoy in their lives. The country's long coastline offers some of the world's most beautiful beaches.

Copacabana section of the beach at Rio de Janeiro

Playing soccer (left) and surfing at the beach (right) are popular in Brazil.

Swimming, surfing, and watching "futeball" (soccer) are favorite national pastimes.

Music, singing, and dancing are part of almost every Brazilian social activity. The most important

event is Carnival, a four-day
holiday that comes every
year before Lent. During
Carnival, Brazilians parade
in beautiful costumes.

In Portuguese, *Bom dia*
means "Good day." It is a

greeting heard everywhere
in Brazil. In spite of their
many problems, Brazilians
have a bright outlook. In
Brazil today the "good days"
are getting better.

WORDS YOU SHOULD KNOW

abolish(uh • BAHL • ish) — to stop; to do away with

allies(AL • ize) — nations united for a cause

cacao(ka • KAH • oh) — seed pods of the cacao tree; the source of chocolate

capital(KAP • ih • til) — the place where a country's government is located

civilian(sih • VILL • yun) — a person who is not a soldier; not a member of the military

constitution(kahn • stih • TOO • shun) — a system of basic laws or rules for the government of a country

export(EX • port) — an item sold and sent to another country

frontier(frun • TEER) — the border of a country or a region

hammock(HAM • uck) — a woven hanging bed

hydroelectric power(HY • droh • ee • LEK • trik powr) — electric power produced by the energy of falling water

import(IM • port) — an item bought in one country and brought into another

independence(in • dih • PEN • dince) — freedom from the control of another country or person

native(NAY • tiv) — born in or belonging to a place

nuclear reactor(NOO • klee • er re • ACK • ter) — a machine that produces energy from the splitting of the nuclei, or centers, of atoms

outpost(OUT • pohst) — a place away from the main centers of activity

pastime(PASS • tyme) — recreation; a way of spending time pleasantly

petroleum(peh • TROH • lee • um) — liquid oil in the earth

plantation(plan • TAY • shun) — a farm, a place for growing crops

pioneer(pye • uh • NEER) — the first settler in a place

pollute(puh • LOOT) — to make dirty

range(RAYNJ) — grassland on which cattle or sheep graze

region(REE • jun) — a large area of a country

remote(rih • MOAT) — distant; far away

republic(rih • PUB • lick) — a country with elected leaders

rights(RYTES) — legal claims protected from challenge or change

rural(ROO • ril) — in or of the country

slavery(SLAY • ver • ee) — the practice of owning people

slum(SLUHM) — an area of rundown or makeshift structures used as living quarters

telegraph(TEL • ih • graf) — an electric wire system used for carrying signals

tropical(TROP • ih • kil) — having to do with the parts of the earth just to the north and south of the equator

unexplored(un • ex • PLORD) — not visited and mapped; unknown

wilderness(WIHL • der • niss) — a region not inhabited by people

INDEX

About the Author

Karen Jacobsen is a graduate of the University of Connecticut and Syracuse University. She has been a teacher and is a writer. She likes to find out about interesting subjects and then write about them.